DINOSAURS RULED!

PTERANODON

LEIGH ROCKWOOD

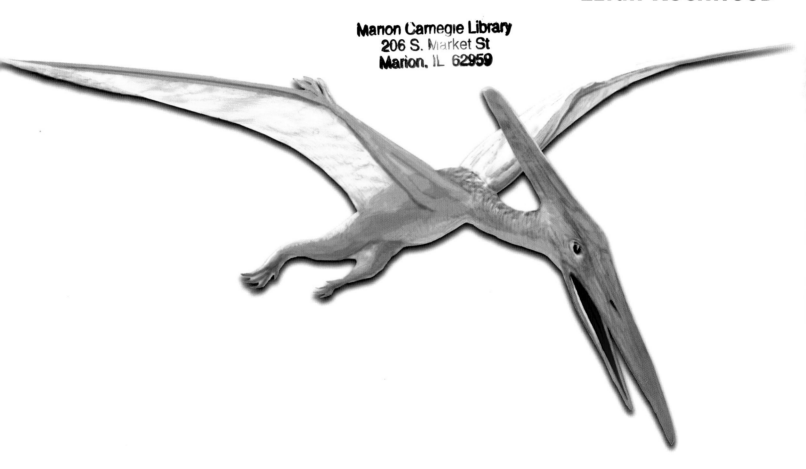

PowerKiDS press.
New York

Published in 2012 by The Rosen Publishing Group, Inc.
29 East 21st Street, New York, NY 10010

First Edition

Editor: Joanne Randolph
Book Design: Kate Laczynski

Photo Credits: Cover, title page by Brian Garvey; cover background (palm tree leaves) © www.iStockphoto.com/dra_schwartz; cover background (palm tree trunk) iStockphoto/Thinkstock; cover background (ginkgo leaves) Hemera/Thinkstock; cover background (fern leaves) Brand X Pictures/Thinkstock; cover background (moss texture) © www.iStockphoto.com/Robert Linton; cover background (sky) © www.iStockphoto.com/konradlew; cover background (mountains), pp. 4–5, 6, 7, 9, 10–11, 12, 13, 14, 15, 16, 17, 18–19, 20–21 © 2011 Orpheus Books Ltd.; p. 8 © www.iStockphoto.com/moodville; p. 22 Antonio Scorza/AFP/Getty Images.

Library of Congress Cataloging-in-Publication Data

Rockwood, Leigh.
 Pteranodon / by Leigh Rockwood. — 1st ed.
    p. cm. — (Dinosaurs ruled!)
Includes index.
 ISBN 978-1-4488-4965-9 (library binding) — ISBN 978-1-4488-5080-8 (pbk.) —
ISBN 978-1-4488-5081-5 (6-pack)
 1. Pteranodon—Juvenile literature. I. Title. II. Series.
 QE862..P7R625 2012
 567.918—dc22

                              2010048084

Manufactured in the United States of America

CPSIA Compliance Information: Batch #WS11PK: For Further Information contact Rosen Publishing, New York, New York at 1-800-237-9932

CONTENTS

MEET THE PTERANODON

Have you heard of the pteranodon? If you thought the pteranodon was a flying dinosaur, you were wrong! It is true that the pteranodon was a prehistoric flying reptile. It is also true that it lived during the age of dinosaurs. The pteranodon was not a dinosaur, though. Flying reptiles such as the pteranodon belonged to a group of animals called pterosaurs. Pterosaurs and dinosaurs were close relatives.

Paleontologists have learned a lot about the pteranodon by studying its **fossils**. For example, they know that the pteranodon had a short tail and a crest on its head.

Scientists know that pteranodons had large wings. They also know that they were toothless. In fact, "pteranodon" means "winged and toothless"!

THE LATE CRETACEOUS PERIOD

Scientists use geologic time to break Earth's long history into smaller time periods. The pteranodon lived during the Late Cretaceous period. This period of geologic time lasted from about 89 to 65 million years ago.

The pteranodon and the rest of the pterosaurs became **extinct** at the end of the Late Cretaceous

Pterosaurs lived alongside many kinds of dinosaurs, such as hadrosaurs, shown here.

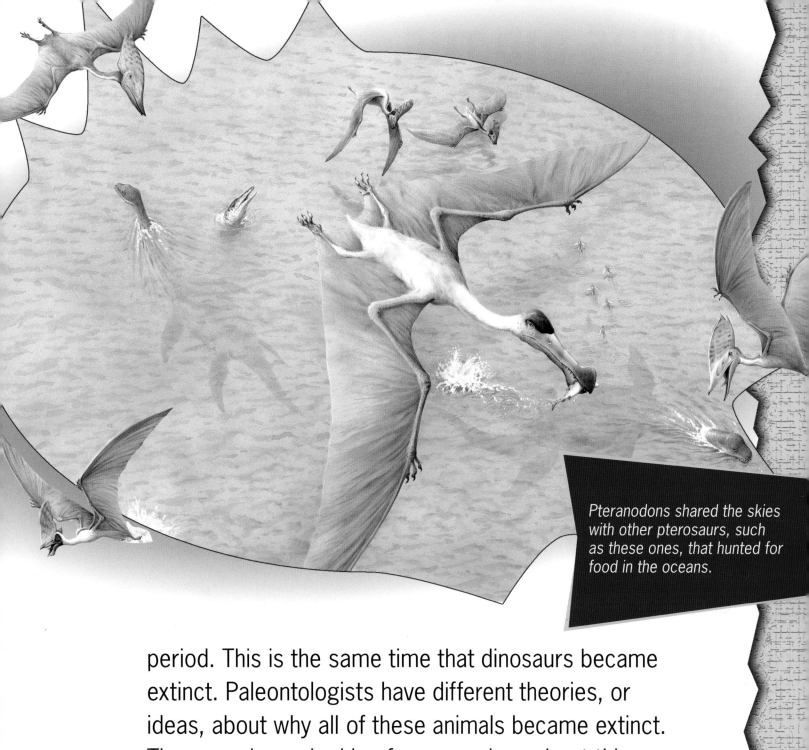

Pteranodons shared the skies with other pterosaurs, such as these ones, that hunted for food in the oceans.

period. This is the same time that dinosaurs became extinct. Paleontologists have different theories, or ideas, about why all of these animals became extinct. They are always looking for more clues about this mass extinction, though.

WHERE DID THE PTERANODON LIVE?

Fossils form in **sedimentary rocks**. These rocks form when sediment such as mud, sand, or stone is under pressure for a very long time. If a dead plant or animal is covered by sediment, its remains may form a fossil.

Pteranodon fossils have been found in Kansas, in North America, and in England, in Europe. During the

Prehistoric oceans shaped these rock formations in Kansas. Pteranodon and other pterosaur fossils have been found here.

The pteranodon likely spent much of its time near water. Some scientists think pteranodons could swim and may have rested on the water as seagulls do today.

Late Cretaceous period both of these continents had a warm and humid **climate**. Pteranodons have been found in sedimentary rocks that formed near oceans and seas. This leads paleontologists to think that pteranodons had a diet and habitat a bit like today's pelicans'.

A FLYING REPTILE

The pteranodon was one of the largest pterosaurs. A fully grown pteranodon had a body that was about 6 feet (2 m) long. The wingspan of a pteranodon this size could be up to about 33 feet (10 m)! The pteranodon was very light for its size. It weighed only around 55 pounds (25 kg). This was in part because pteranodons had hollow bones, as do today's birds.

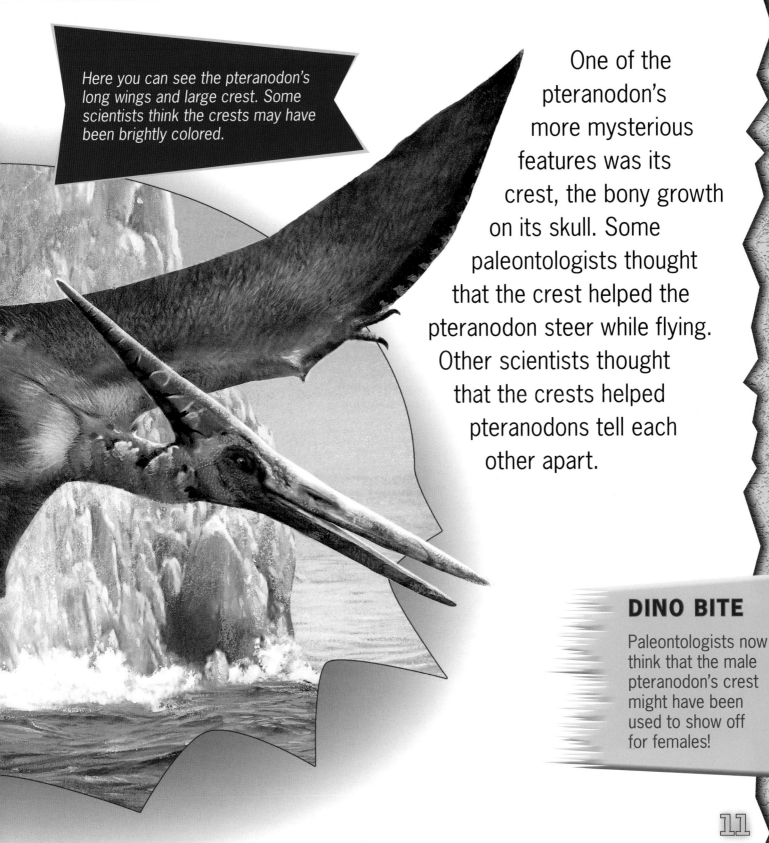

Here you can see the pteranodon's long wings and large crest. Some scientists think the crests may have been brightly colored.

One of the pteranodon's more mysterious features was its crest, the bony growth on its skull. Some paleontologists thought that the crest helped the pteranodon steer while flying. Other scientists thought that the crests helped pteranodons tell each other apart.

DINO BITE

Paleontologists now think that the male pteranodon's crest might have been used to show off for females!

PTERANODON WINGS

Paleontologists think that the pteranodon was a strong flier. They came to this theory by looking closely at fossils of its wings. They saw that the pteranodon's wings and shoulders would have been very muscular. Due to the size of its body and its wings, it would have

The pteranodon could use its wings to flap or to glide over the ocean's surface. It also folded them to walk on all fours while on land.

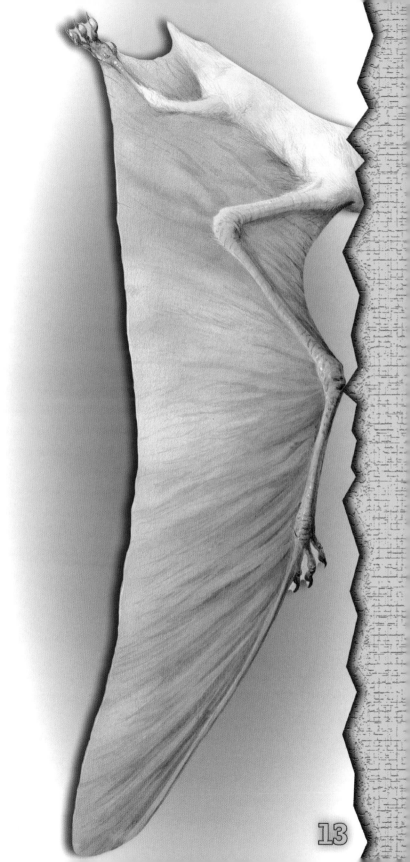

been hard for the pteranodon to flap its wings quickly. This means that it pushed itself through the air with large, slow flaps of its wings instead.

Although it flew, the pteranodon did not have feathers, as a bird does. Dinosaurs are more closely related to today's birds than pteranodons are.

PTERANODON SENSES

Sharp vision helped the pteranodon see fish moving under the water.

The pteranodon had a large head. It also had a large brain compared to the size of the rest of its body. Fossils of the pteranodon's skull show that its brain was likely much like that of some of today's birds. Based on this clue, paleontologists think that the pterosaur was fairly smart and had good eyesight. They think the pteranodon may have had a good sense of smell, too. This is also true of many birds today that eat fish or hunt for **prey**. Sharp senses and intelligence would have been useful to the pteranodon as it hunted for food in the prehistoric oceans.

Scientists think that the pteranodon's wings could sense changes in wind and other forces around them. This helped pteranodons fly with great skill.

EATING ON THE FLY

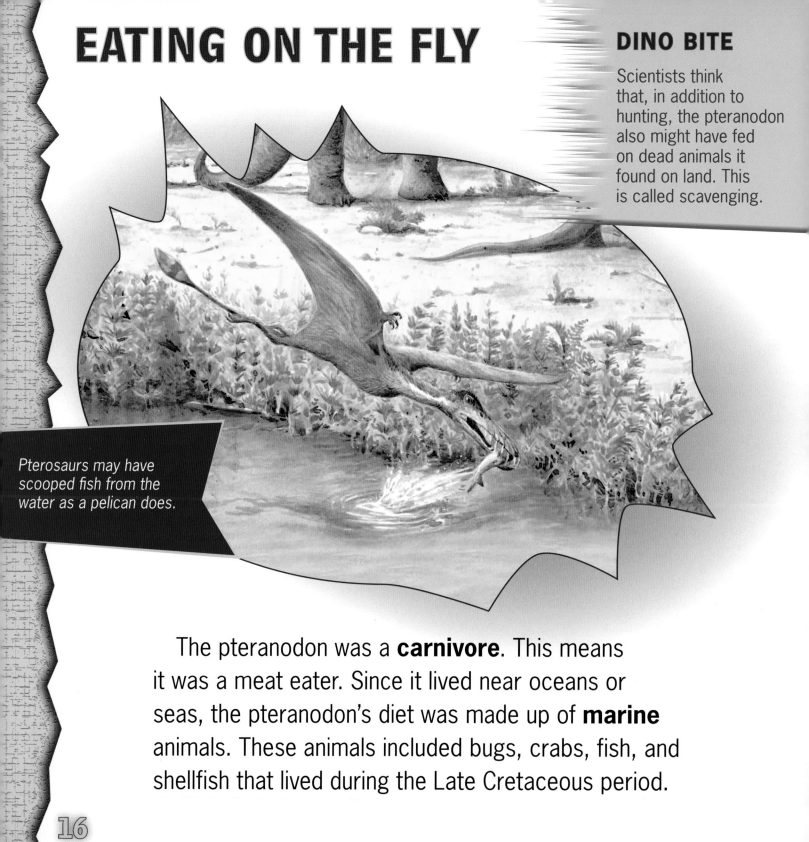

Pterosaurs may have scooped fish from the water as a pelican does.

The pteranodon was a **carnivore**. This means it was a meat eater. Since it lived near oceans or seas, the pteranodon's diet was made up of **marine** animals. These animals included bugs, crabs, fish, and shellfish that lived during the Late Cretaceous period.

The pteranodon had no teeth. How then did it hunt and eat? Paleontologists think that the pterosaur scooped its prey out of the water using its beaklike mouth. It would then swallow its food whole. This way of hunting and eating might have looked a lot like the way today's pelicans hunt and eat.

If the pteranodon scavenged for dead animals, it might have kept its eyes open for animals that were about to be killed. It could come back to eat them once the other predators left.

MALES AND FEMALES

Fossils give paleontologists many clues about an animal. They use this information to come up with theories about that animal's life.

When paleontologists look at pteranodon fossils, they can see that females had bigger hips than males. This is because pteranodons likely laid eggs, just as other dinosaurs and today's reptiles and birds do. Paleontologists also saw that males

Can you see that the crest on the pteranodon on the right is smaller than those on the other two? Females had smaller crests than males did. However, not all males' crests were the same size either.

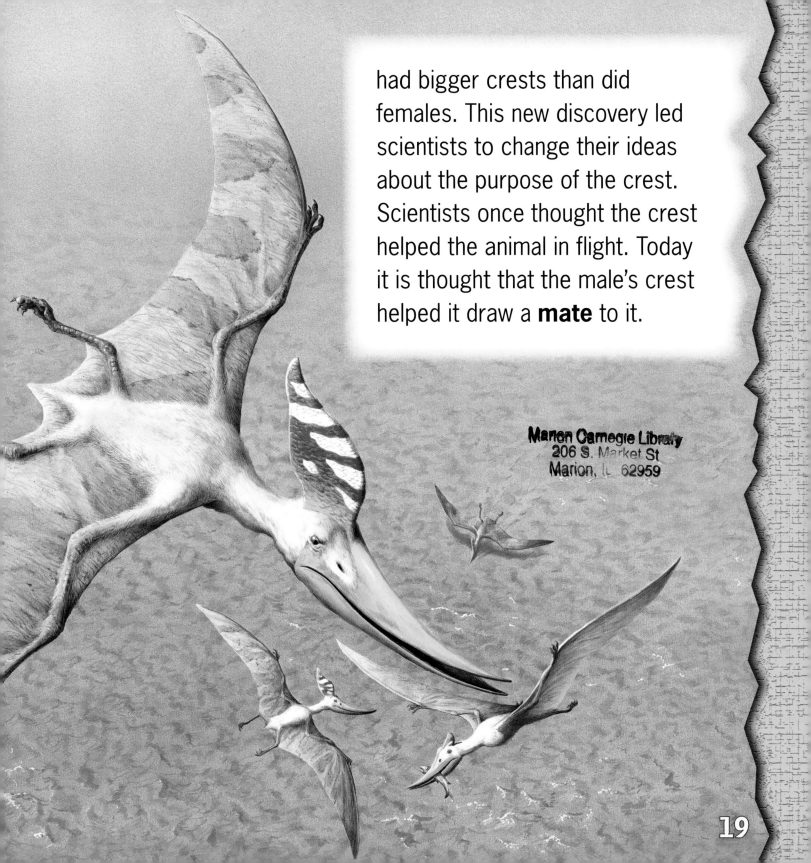

had bigger crests than did females. This new discovery led scientists to change their ideas about the purpose of the crest. Scientists once thought the crest helped the animal in flight. Today it is thought that the male's crest helped it draw a **mate** to it.

OUT OF REACH

The pteranodon was a predator, but other animals also hunted it. One of its dinosaur predators was *Tyrannosaurus rex*, one of the most fearsome carnivores of the Late Cretaceous period.

The pteranodon had claws on its wings. It was not big enough to fight predators like a 6-ton (5 t) T. rex, though.

Pteranodons would have been safe from predators like T. rex if they stayed in the air. Once they landed, though, they were fair game for this fearsome hunter.

The pteranodon's best **defense** against its predators was to fly away. In fact, paleontologists think that the pteranodon spent a great deal of time in the air. It may have landed only to nest, sleep, and mate.

NO BONES ABOUT IT

The first pteranodon fossil was found in 1876 in Kansas. It was a skull dug up by S. W. Williston, a fossil collector who worked for the paleontologist Othniel Marsh.

Here a paleontologist presents a new pterosaur skeleton at a conference in Brazil.

More pteranodon fossils have been found since then. You may remember that the pteranodon had hollow bones. Their bones were often crushed before they could fossilize. For that reason, most pteranodon fossils have been found in places where there was once water. The soft ocean floor **protected** the pteranodon's bones enough that fossils could form. Each new fossil that is found can tell scientists new things about the pteranodon's life.

GLOSSARY

carnivore (KAHR-neh-vor) An animal that eats other animals.

climate (KLY-mut) The kind of weather a certain place has.

defense (dih-FENTS) Something a living thing does that helps keep it safe.

extinct (ik-STINGKT) No longer existing.

fossils (FO-sulz) The hardened remains of dead animals or plants.

marine (muh-REEN) Having to do with the sea.

mate (MAYT) A partner for making babies.

paleontologists (pay-lee-on-TAH-luh-jists) People who study things that lived in the past.

prey (PRAY) An animal that is hunted by another animal for food.

protected (pruh-TEKT-ed) Kept safe.

sedimentary rocks (seh-deh-MEN-teh-ree ROKS) Stones, sand, or mud that has been pressed together to form rock.

INDEX

B
bones, 10, 22

C
carnivore(s), 16, 20
clue(s), 7, 14, 18
crest(s), 4, 11, 19

D
defense, 21

E
extinction, 7

F
fossil(s), 4, 8, 12, 14,
     18, 22

G
geologic time, 6
group, 4

H
head, 4, 14
history, 6

I
ideas, 7, 19

M
mate, 19

O
oceans, 9, 15–16

P
paleontologist(s), 4, 7, 9,
     11–12, 14, 17–18, 21–22
prey, 15, 17
pterosaur(s), 4, 6, 10, 15, 17

R
relatives, 4
reptile(s), 4, 18

S
scientists, 6, 11, 19, 22
sedimentary rocks, 8–9

T
tail, 4
theories, 7, 12, 18

WEB SITES

Due to the changing nature of Internet links, PowerKids Press has developed an online list of Web sites related to the subject of this book. This site is updated regularly. Please use this link to access the list:
www.powerkidslinks.com/dinr/pteran/